New York Fish Species

Game Fish & Panfish

Billy Grinslott & Kinsey Marie Books

ISBN - 9781968228521

I0025417

Longear Sunfish Northern Sunfish are small, thin-bodied fish with a unique long ear flap on their gill cover, that how they got their name long ear. They are often mistaken for a pumpkinseed. They have an olive to rusty-brown back, a bright orange belly. They typically reach a length of 4.5 inches. They are mostly active during the day and inactive at night.

The Green Sunfish is blue green in color. It has yellow flecks on both its scales and some parts of its sides. The Green Sunfish also has broken blue stripes which is why some people confuse it with the Bluegill. Green Sunfish are very adaptable. They can live in any body of water that has vegetation or weeds. Green sunfish are opportunistic feeders, consuming insects, small fish, and other invertebrates.

The Warmouth is a member of the Rock Bass, Green Sunfish and Bluegill family. They can survive in low oxygen environments while other fish cannot. Warmouth can thrive in muddy water, when other fish can't. Warmouth are often confused with rock bass. The difference between the two is in the anal fin: warmouth have three spines on the anal fin ray and rock bass have six spines.

The bluegill also considered a sunfish is the most popular fish to fish for. They are called pan fish because they are about the size of a frying pan. Bluegills love to eat insects and bugs. They have good vision and rely on their keen eyesight to feed. Three types in this group are the Bluegill, Sunfish, and Pumpkinseed.

The Redbreast sunfish has a red-yellow chest and belly with rusty brown spots on their body. The species is known for its distinctive grunting vocalizations, which are produced by grinding their teeth together. Redbreast sunfish can survive in oxygen-poor environments by using their gills to extract oxygen from air bubbles trapped in aquatic vegetation.

The Pumpkinseed is also known as pond perch, sun perch, and punky's sunfish. It can be found in numerous lakes, ponds, and rivers. It is their body shape resembling the seed of a pumpkin, that inspired their name. Pumpkinseed sunfish have speckles on their orangish colored sides and back, with a yellow to orange belly and chest. They are active during the day and rest at night near the bottom or in shelter areas.

White perch grow seven to ten inches in length and rarely weigh more than one pound. They have a silvery body with faint lines on the sides. The white perch is an opportunistic feeder. Young feed primarily on zooplankton and adults feed on aquatic insect larvae, minnows and fish eggs. White Perch is a euryhaline species, inhabiting fresh, brackish and coastal waters. The biggest white perch ever caught in New York State is a 3-pound, 4-ounces.

The two most famous perches are the common perch and the yellow perch. The yellow perch has a brilliant greenish yellow color with orange fins. The yellow perch is the biggest one and can grow to a size of 18 inches. It's also known as the jumbo perch. The other type of perch is the white perch. The official New York State record yellow perch weighed 3 lbs. 8 oz.

The Rock Bass is not actually a bass but a member of the sunfish family. The biggest Rock Bass ever caught on record weighs about three pounds and was a little over one foot long. Rock bass like waters with rocky vegetated areas, that's how they got their name.

There are two main types of crappies. The white crappie and the black crappie. They are also members of the sunfish family. The difference between the white and black crappie is one has dark spots and the other has dark lines and is lighter in color. The white crappie has six dorsal fin spines, whereas the black crappie has eight dorsal fin spines. The white crappie can grow bigger and more of the bigger white crappie are caught in North America. The biggest white crappie ever caught in New York State weighed 4 lb. 7 oz. (19 inches long).

The sucker fish has the same mouth as a carp. They got their name because their mouth is like a suction cup. They normally are bottom feeders and suck their food from the bottom of the lake. Many people use sucker fish to fish for northern pike and other big game fish. The largest white sucker ever caught in New York State weighed 5 pounds, 8 ounces.

The black, brown and yellow bullhead are part of the catfish family. They usually only grow to about 10 inches long. They use their whiskers to help find food. The bullhead is the most common member of the catfish family. Bullheads live in the water containing low oxygen levels. They can survive on low oxygen areas, where other fish can't. The biggest brown bullhead ever caught in New York State weighed 7 pounds, 6 ounces.

Flathead Catfish, their body is wide but flattened and very low in height. Both eyes are on the top of the flattened head, giving excellent vision to see upward. Flathead catfish live mainly in large bodies of water like big rivers and reservoirs. They prefer deep pools of water. Flathead catfish can grow to be over 60 pounds in weight.

The Channel Catfish are the most fished catfish species with around 8 million anglers fishing for them per year. Channel catfish have taste buds all over their body, making them highly sensitive to the taste and smell of food. They also have barbels (whiskers) around their mouths, which are used for sensing and tasting food. They use sound waves to communicate with each other. They can also produce alarm substances to warn other catfish of danger. The biggest channel catfish ever caught in New York State is a 37-pound 9-ounces.

The stonecat is a slender, freshwater catfish known for its preference for living in fast moving streams and rivers. They are often found under rocks and boulders in riffles. Stonecats have a long, thin body with a rounded or slightly forked tail. Their color varies, typically ranging from tan to gray on the back and sides, with a lighter belly. Stonecats are primarily active at night, feeding on insects, fish eggs, and small fish.

White catfish are interesting because they are smaller than other common catfish species like channel catfish, they have a wider head and lack the black spots of channel catfish. White catfish are the smallest of the large North American catfish species. The White catfish has white chin barbells, which distinguish it from other species. There are four pairs of barbels, whiskers around the mouth, two on the chin, one at the angle of the mouth, and one behind the nostril.

Bowfins can breathe both air and water, putting them at an advantage in low-oxygen waters. Bowfins are often described as prehistoric relics. This is because species can be traced to fossils from the Cretaceous, Eocene and Jurassic period. The biggest Bowfin ever caught in New York State weighed 13 pounds, 8 ounces.

White Bass or striped bass range in color from a silvery white to a pale green. Their backs are mostly black, while their sides and belly are pale with stripes running along them. White Bass are related to Striped Bass and called wipers. The official New York State record for White Bass is a 3 lb. 8 oz. fish.

Striped bass are often called Stripers. Striped bass live in both salt and fresh water. Striped bass have very sensitive eyes and will seek deep water when the sun is out. Striped bass have a preferred water temperature range of from 55° F to 68° F, and swim to find water of these temperatures. White Bass are related to Striped Bass and have lighter stripes on their sides. The largest striped bass ever caught in New York State waters is a 76-pound fish.

Lake whitefish are related to salmon and trout. They are known for their deep-bodied, silvery appearance and are a major part of the Great Lakes ecosystem. They typically grow to 17-22 inches and range from 1.5-10 pounds. Whitefish are a popular and valuable commercial fish, generating the greatest income for Great Lakes commercial fisheries. Lake whitefish are also known as Lake Superior whitefish, whiting, and shad. The biggest Lake whitefish ever caught in New York State was a 10-pound, 8-ounce fish.

The burbot, also known as the eel pout. They get their name because they have a serpent-like or eel-like body. They can wrap their tail around things. There's nothing to worry about if you catch one, they may try to wrap their tail around your arm, but they are harmless. Burbots are adapted to cold water and are found in large, cold rivers, lakes, and reservoirs, primarily preferring freshwater habitats. Burbots are also known as ling, cusk, or eelpout. The largest burbot ever caught in New York State weighed 16 pounds, 12 ounces.

Lake Sturgeons have sharp spines on their back, so be careful when handling them. Instead of scales, sturgeon skin is covered in bony plates called scutes, which can be very sharp on young sturgeon. Sturgeons have been around since the dinosaur days. Sturgeons mostly live in large, freshwater lakes and rivers. Their average lifespan is 50 to 60 years. The largest Lake Sturgeon documented in New York State is a 159.4-pound, 73.6-inch fish.

There are few different species of Gar, the Longnose gar, Short nose and Alligator gar. The Long Nose Gar got its name because of its long mouth that looks like an alligator's mouth. The alligator gar is one of the biggest freshwater fish growing up to 10 feet long. The world record for a catch was set at 327 pounds. The biggest longnose gar ever caught in New York State was a 15-pound, 14-ounce fish.

Snakehead fish are known as walking fish, because they can move on land for days by wiggling with their fins and body. They can breathe air with lung-like organs, allowing them to survive out of water for days and even crawl to new water bodies using their fins. They can also burrow into the mud and hibernate during cold weather or dry spells. They thrive in various slow-moving, shallow, vegetated waters, like ponds, swamps, and streams, and can survive in low oxygen levels.

Male freshwater drum also known as sheepshead make a rumbling or grunting sound by contracting muscles along their air bladder walls. They have large, ivory-like ear bones that can be up to an inch in diameter, which Native Americans used as necklaces or bracelets and sometimes referred to as the lucky stones. Freshwater drum are primarily bottom feeders, spending much of their time near the bottom of lakes and rivers in search of food. The biggest freshwater drum ever caught in New York State weighed 36 pounds.

Carp have long been an important food fish to humans. Carp are bottom feeders for the most part and their mouth is made like a suction cup, so they can suck food off the bottom. Carp are good for a lake because they help clean the bottom of the lake. The biggest common carp ever caught in New York State weighed 50 pounds 6 ounces.

The rainbow trout gets its name because of its brilliant colors. Rainbow trout populations are good indicators of water pollution because they can only survive in clean waters. They like to live in rivers and streams. Rainbow trout rank among the top five most sought game fish in North America. The largest rainbow trout ever caught in New York State weighed 31 pounds, 3 ounces.

The lake trout is one of the biggest of the trout family. The biggest lake trout caught was 72 pounds. Lake trout like to live in lakes that are deep. They like being in the cool water in the deep parts of a lake. They have been reported to live up to 70 years in some Canadian lakes. The biggest lake trout ever caught in New York State weighed 41 pounds, 8 ounces.

Brook trout are characterized by their olive-green bodies with pale, worm-like markings, red spots with bluish halos, and orange-red fins with white and black edges. They can grow up to 12 inches in length. Brook trout are cold-water fish that prefer clean, clear, and cold streams, lakes, and ponds. The biggest brook trout ever caught in New York State is 6-pounds, 3-ounces.

Chinook also known as the king salmon are the most widespread Salmon in North America. Chinook salmon are hatch in freshwater streams and rivers then migrate out to the saltwater environment of the ocean to feed and grow. Chinook salmon are the largest of the Pacific Ocean salmon, that's how they got the name king salmon. The biggest Chinook (King) salmon ever caught in New York State weighed 47 pounds and 13 ounces.

Brown trout can live up to 20 years. Brown trout have higher tolerance for warmer waters than either brook or rainbow trout. Brown trout can be found on almost every continent except Antarctica, and many can be found living in the ocean. The largest brown trout ever caught in New York State weighed 34.42 pounds.

Coho salmon, also known as silver salmon, are fish that live in both freshwater and saltwater, migrating from the ocean to their natal streams to spawn, where they die shortly after. Some coho salmon migrate more than 1,000 miles in the ocean, while others remain in marine areas close to the streams where they were born. Adult coho salmon typically weigh 8 to 12 pounds and are 24 to 30 inches long, but some can reach up to 36 pounds. The biggest Coho salmon ever caught in New York State weighed 33 pounds, 4 ounces.

The largemouth bass is the most sought-after bass in North America. Largemouth bass live in just about every lake in North America. They have great hearing and can hear a crayfish crawling on the bottom of the lake. The biggest largemouth bass ever caught in New York State weighed 12 pounds, 6 ounces.

Smallmouth bass have a smaller mouth than the largemouth bass. They also have different markings and are lighter in color. They don't live in most lakes because they prefer living in colder water. They are typically found in the northern states in America because the water is cooler. The current world record smallmouth is an 11-pound, 15-ounce fish. They can be found in lakes, reservoirs, and rivers. The biggest Smallmouth bass ever caught in New York State is a 9-pound fish.

The sauger is part of the walleye family. There are 2 different types of saugers. The normal sauger and the suageye. The saugeye is a mix of the sauger and walleye. The suageye have white eyes just like the walleye. The sauger and suageye are smaller than the walleye. Saugers are more likely to be found in large rivers with deep pools but are also found in lakes. The world-record sauger weighed 8 lbs. 12 oz.

The walleye got its name because of its white looking eyes. Their eyes collect light, even in low light conditions. This means they can see in the dark. Because they can see in the dark, they mostly feed at night. During the daytime their eyes are very sensitive, so they usually head for deeper water or shady places. Walleye like to live in cooler water and are normally found in the upper part of North America. The biggest walleye ever caught in New York State weighed 18 pounds, 2 ounces.

Pickerel kind of look like northern pike, but they are not. The Pike is larger in size than the Pickerel. The Pickerel has more spots than the Pike, but the Pike has spots on its fins and pickerel don't. Pickerel has a dark bar beneath their eyes and northern pike don't. Pickerel are also known as gunfish or slime darts. The biggest Chain Pickerel ever caught in New York State weighed 8 pounds. 1 ounce.

The Northern Pike is one of the most sought-after fish for anglers. It got its name because it likes to live in cooler water mainly in the northern states of North America. The northern pike is a very aggressive predator. They don't like to live in groups with other fish, they are very territorial and like to live alone. Their behavior is closely affected by weather conditions. The biggest Northern Pike ever caught in New York State weighed 46 pounds, 2 ounces.

The muskellunge called the Musky or Muskie for short is one of the biggest game fish in freshwater lakes. The largest on record was 69 pounds, 15 ounces. The Muskie likes to live in cooler water and can be found in most lakes in the upper part of north America. Anglers look at Muskellunges as trophy fish. They are hard to catch. There's a saying that it takes a thousand casts to catch one. The largest muskellunge officially recognized in New York State is a 69-pound, 15-ounce fish.

Another breed of the Muskie is the tiger muskie. The tiger muskie is a cross between the northern pike and muskie. They grow larger and faster than normal muskies and northern pikes. The tiger muskie got its name because it has tiger like stripes. Tiger Muskies are very rare and hard to catch. The world record tiger muskie is a massive fish weighing 51 pounds, 3 ounces. The official New York State record for the largest tiger muskie is a 35-pound, 8-ounce fish.

Steelhead are rainbow trout that migrate to the ocean and then return to their freshwater spawning grounds. Steelhead and rainbow trout are genetically identical, the difference lies in their lifestyle, with steelhead migrating to the ocean and rainbow trout remaining in freshwater. The biggest steelhead (rainbow trout) ever caught in New York State weighed 31 pounds 3 ounces.

Atlantic salmon are anadromous, meaning they live in both freshwater and saltwater. Atlantic Salmon are present in New York State, primarily as landlocked fish in inland lakes and tributaries rather than sea-run fish. They are known for their impressive leaping abilities, allowing them to jump over waterfalls and obstacles to reach spawning grounds. Atlantic salmon change color when they return to freshwater to spawn, becoming a rusty-bronze color with red markings. The largest Atlantic salmon caught in New York, was a 27-inch-long fish.

Fun Facts About New York Fish

1 - Official State Fish: The brook trout (native) is the freshwater symbol, while the striped bass is the official marine fish.

2 - Unlike other salmon, the brook trout lack teeth on the roof of their mouth. They rely on their bottom teeth to grab food.

3 - The lake sturgeon is the granddaddy of all fish. They can live up to 100 years and weigh up to 300 pounds.

4 - A 70-lb muskie and a 46-lb northern pike are top, historical records for New York freshwater fish.

5 - Key game fish include largemouth/smallmouth bass, walleye, northern pike, and various trout (brook, brown, rainbow).

6 - The burbot, also known as eelpout, is a member of the freshwater cod family and has an odd habit of wrapping its slimy tail around the hand or arm of anglers.

7 – World record fish have been caught in New York, with major records including a 76-pound striped bass, a 46 lb. 2 oz northern pike.

Author Page

Billy Grinslott & Kinsey Marie Books

Copyright, All Rights Reserved

ISBN – 9781968228521

Thanks

www.ingramcontent.com/pod-product-compliance
Lightning Source LLC
Chambersburg PA
CBHW060849270326
41934CB00002B/53

9 781968 228521